POLLUTION

REDBACK publishing

Redback Publishing
PO Box 357 Frenchs Forest NSW 2086
Australia

www.redbackpublishing.com.au
orders@redbackpublishing.com.au

First Published 2020
Reprinted 2022

978-1-922322-01-2

Author: Peter Turner
Editor: Caroline Thomas
Designer: Redback Publishing

Originated by Redback Publishing

Printed and bound in Malaysia

Acknowledgements
Abbreviations: l—left, r—right, b—bottom, t—top, c—centre, m—middle
We would like to thank the following for permission to reproduce photographs: (Images © shutterstock),

NATIONAL LIBRARY OF AUSTRALIA
A catalogue record for this book is available from the National Library of Australia

CONTENTS

WHAT IS POLLUTION?

Pollution is something that causes harm to an area of the natural environment, such as the air, soil or water. When damaging substances such as chemicals and waste products cause pollution, those substances are referred to as pollutants. Pollution can come from nature, but is mostly produced by humans.

Pollution is a problem that requires rapid solutions, both within Australia and internationally, due to the growing human population and the increasing size of cities. Pollution can often be invisible, but still dangerous for our health and our planet.

MODERN CITIES

As cities have grown in size to become major centres of industry, commerce and population, they have also become major pollution centres. Motor vehicles, factories and power plants produce huge quantities of pollutants in large cities every single day. The gases produced become concentrated in the atmosphere around the city and can have a negative effect on the health of the people living there.

NATURAL POLLUTANTS

In Australia, the most common example of natural pollution is the smoke from bushfires. This smoke contains large quantities of ash, soot and carbon dioxide which make breathing difficult. If humans or animals become caught in an area where the smoke is dense, they can suffocate.

Flooding can cause dangerous objects to be swept into our waterways, while subsiding floodwaters can become stagnant and contain waterborne pests and diseases that are dangerous to humans, animals and plants.

Overseas, volcanic eruptions can spew out lava that is filled with toxic gases which are a natural cause of acid rain.

Hurricanes and cyclones can lift up soils and carry their stored toxins over long distances before dumping them.

A GLOBAL PROBLEM

Pollution is a global problem. Air and water pollution can travel to other countries, a long way from their original source. Toxic smog can travel through the air from one country to its neighbours.

POLLUTION IN AUSTRALIA

The results of a two-year study by The Lancet Commission on Pollution and Health showed that pollution is responsible for an estimated nine million premature deaths. It is the largest environmental cause of death and disease in the world.

AIR POLLUTION

Air pollution is responsible for causing 3,000 premature deaths in Australia each year.

SALINITY

Approximately 30% of agricultural land in Australia is severely degraded by salinity.

HAZARDOUS WASTE

85% of Australian households put hazardous waste such as light bulbs and chemicals in the rubbish bin.

PLASTIC FRAGMENTS

One million seabirds and over 100,000 marine mammals die each year because of plastics. One square kilometre of Australian ocean contains 4,000 fragments of plastic.

WATER USE

Every Australian resident uses an average of 341,000 litres of water per year.

PLASTIC BAGS

A single plastic bag has a life expectancy of 1,000 years. Australians use approximately four billion plastic bags per year.

LAND POLLUTION

Land pollution leads to 80% of all marine and freshwater pollution.

HISTORY OF POLLUTION

Pollution has not always been the significant global problem that it is today. There have always been natural sources of pollution, but humans have generated so much pollution that it has sometimes proven deadly.

INDUSTRIAL REVOLUTION

Many of today's pollution problems can be traced back to the 19th century when humans discovered that energy could be generated by burning coal. This revolutionised the way that humans could work and live.

The introduction of powered machinery transformed the output level of factories. Products that were previously made by hand now became mass produced, before being transported to large numbers of new buyers and customers.

Rural areas gave way to industrial cities that quickly spread across the once green lands. It took a long time to realise that burning coal produced many toxins that were dangerous to the factory workers and city dwellers.

The industrial revolution forever changed the way that humans lived.

THE OZONE LAYER

The ozone layer is an important part of the Earth's upper atmosphere. It acts as a shield, helping to prevent the sun's harmful ultraviolet rays from reaching the Earth.

The first clear evidence of ozone depletion became news in 1984, when scientists discovered a large area over Antarctica with very little ozone at all, giving rise to the name the 'ozone hole'. It is not actually a hole, but represents a thinning of the ozone layer each year over Antarctica, South America and southern Australia.

The ozone layer is highly sensitive and has been partly destroyed by the effects of chlorofluorocarbons (CFCs), artificial greenhouse gases used in aerosol cans, refrigerators, foam and some air conditioners. When CFCs rise in the atmosphere, they release gases that destroy ozone.

In 1989, an international treaty, called the Montreal Protocol, was enforced to eliminate the use of CFCs, in order to reduce the damage to the ozone layer.

!

September 2017 marked the 30 year anniversary of the Montreal Protocol. Now acknowledged as a success, the treaty is slowly but surely reversing the damage done to the ozone layer.

PLASTICS

Plastics affect every living organism on Earth. Plastic pollution includes whole pieces of plastic litter, microplastics that are under five millimetres wide, and nanoplastics that are too small for humans to see.

!

It is estimated that most humans consume up to five grams of plastic every day. Nanoplastics are present in our tap and bottled water, in fish and seafood, in sea salt, in processed foods and in the dust that attaches to food before we eat it.

THE LIFE CYCLE OF PLASTIC

Nanoplastics in our soils affect plant growth of human food crops and wild animal food sources. Plastics collect in our waterways and treatment plants that discharge into the sea. Once micro and nanoplastics enter our water cycle they can travel the globe, falling as rain in the Amazon and snow in the Antarctic. Microplastics have been found on Mount Everest, our Earth's highest peak and in the Marianna Trench, the deepest point of our ocean.

CREATING NANOPLASTICS

Some microplastics are created intentionally, as small beads in cleaning products, craft items such as glitter, and plastic clothing fibres. Most microplastics come from larger pieces that have broken down into smaller fragments. These smaller fragments gradually degrade into nanoplastics.

!

Clothing, soft furnishings and carpets release tiny plastic fibres into the air we breathe. Every time we wash nylon, lycra and other plastic clothing, microplastics wash into our waterways.

Vehicles on our roads leave tiny fragments of their tyres behind. These pieces wash into our soil, rivers and oceans.

SOFT PLASTICS

Soft plastics are any plastic that can be scrunched into a ball, such as bread bags, chocolate wrappers, cling film, cereal box liners and bubble wrap. Whilst these plastics cannot be recycled with hard plastics because they tangle in the machinery, they can be recycled separately.

Most supermarkets provide places to leave bags of scrunched up soft plastics. They are melted down through a different process before being blended with harder plastics and used to make new products.

NUCLEAR WASTE

The process of generating nuclear power produces one of the most toxic pollutants on the planet - radioactive waste. It can cause serious disease and even death in humans and animals, as well as major environmental damage.

Radioactive waste remains highly toxic for more than 10,000 years. It must be securely stored for the safety of both current and future generations.

FUKUSHIMA

In March 2011, a massive earthquake in Japan triggered a devastating tsunami. The tsunami disabled the power supply and cooling systems at three Fukushima Daiichi reactors, causing a serious nuclear incident.

!

The Chernobyl disaster released 400 times more radiation into the Earth's atmosphere that the dropping of atomic bombs in Hiroshima in 1945.

CHERNOBYL

In 1986, the nuclear power plant at Chernobyl, Ukraine, in central Eastern Europe suffered a massive explosion that caused highly radioactive particles to enter the air, ground and waterways. A cloud of dangerous radioactive pollution spread outwards from Chernobyl to a radius of almost 3,000 kilometres. Winds carried the radioactive particles across Europe as far as Iceland and Greece.

Severe agricultural contamination affected many European locations, including Scandinavia and Britain, for many years after the incident. Many crops and grazing animals were found to have absorbed large amounts of radioactivity, making them unsuitable for human consumption. Today, more than 30 years later, some European land is still contaminated.

AIR POLLUTION

SMOG

Many large cities around the world are badly affected by smog, a visible form of air pollution that often looks like a brownish-yellow cloud. Smog is caused when heat and sunlight combine with air pollutants.

Smog can be caused by the combination of smoke and fog, but these days it is more likely to be caused by a combination of nitrogen oxides, hydrocarbons and sunlight. This is known as photochemical smog and it usually occurs in summer.

AIR POLLUTION

The main sources of air pollution are power stations, factories and motor vehicles. When fossil fuels burn, they produce a number of dangerous chemicals, including sulphur dioxide, nitrogen oxides, carbon monoxide and small toxic particles. These chemicals pollute our atmosphere and are the main cause of acid rain.

!

Smog can be bad for people who suffer from asthma or other lung conditions and can be very dangerous to human health over long periods of time.

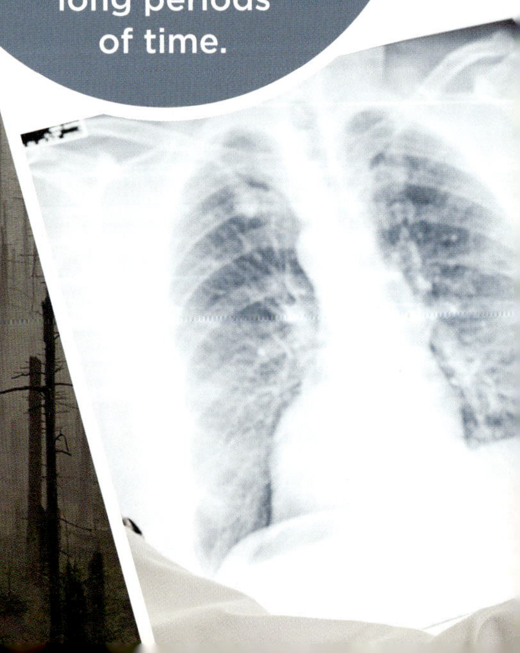

CITY LIVING

Air pollution can cause immediate and long-term health effects in humans. In large cities, there are numerous airborne pollutants that can irritate our throat and eyes, or cause asthma. Breathing in these pollutants can damage our lungs, weaken our immune system and even cause cancer.

!

Regularly opening windows, using an indoor air filter and having indoor plants are ways to reduce the impact of indoor pollution on human health.

INDOOR AIR

Sometimes, indoor air quality can be toxic. Exposure to high levels of pollutants from synthetic building materials, paints, carpets and new furniture can be dangerous to human health.

New homes or renovations generally emit the most toxins, as toxic emissions from a product tend to decrease over time. Some new homes produce many times the maximum allowable limits of some indoor air pollutants.

FRESHWATER POLLUTION

Like air pollution, water pollution can be invisible too. Rivers, lakes and streams may look dirty because mud or silt are stirred up from the bottom, while a clear, sparkling waterway may contain toxins that can be dangerous to human, animal and plant life.

CHEMICALS AND BACTERIA

Chemical pollutants can affect the amount of oxygen in a waterway, destroy nutrients in the water or even change the colour, taste or temperature of a waterway. This can alter the water to favour certain animal and plant species, or it can have the effect of poisoning the entire waterway and everything in it.

Bacterial pollution, coming from poor sanitation or from untreated sewage released into waterways, can spread very quickly. This can cause serious diseases in those who drink the water or bathe in it.

GROUNDWATER POLLUTION

Groundwater flows deep below the Earth's surface in many parts of Australia. Toxins in soil, particularly near landfill, toxic waste sites or sewage treatment plants, can filter down into the groundwater, along with fertilisers and animal manures. The water may travel long distances over time, transporting the pollution to larger water sources such as lakes, rivers and the ocean.

PHYSICAL POLLUTANTS

Litter, including plastic bags, bottles, cans and shopping trolleys, is a highly visible form of water pollution. When it rains, litter dropped in the streets is often carried into stormwater drains that commonly lead to nearby waterways. Litter can block out sunlight so that plants in the water cannot produce the oxygen for fish to use. Fish, birds and other animals can also get caught in litter and be seriously injured or killed.

MARINE POLLUTION

Over 70 per cent of the Earth's surface is water and our seas and oceans have an enormous influence on our environment. Ocean currents can shift dangerous pollution hundreds of kilometres from its original source.

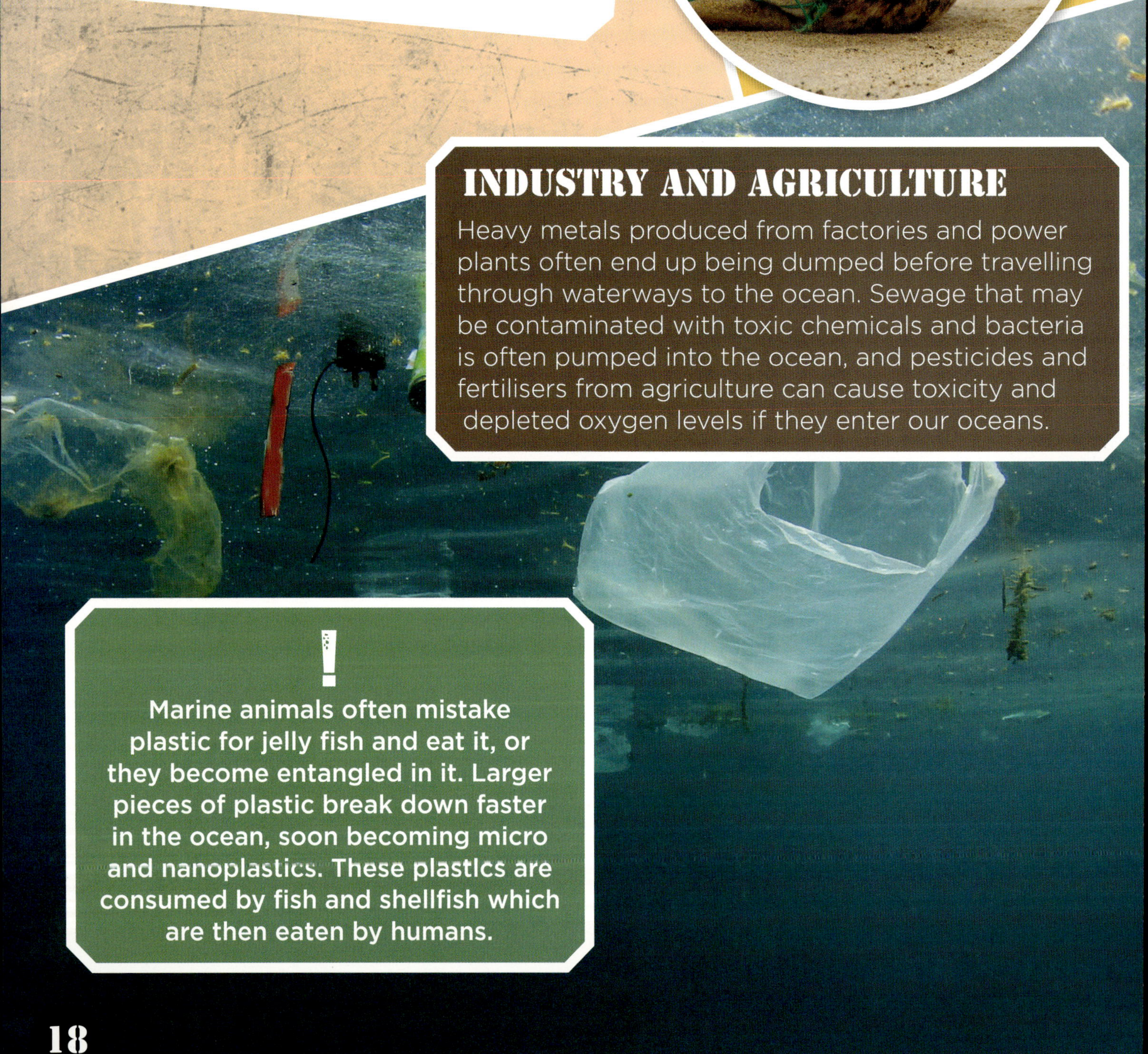

INDUSTRY AND AGRICULTURE

Heavy metals produced from factories and power plants often end up being dumped before travelling through waterways to the ocean. Sewage that may be contaminated with toxic chemicals and bacteria is often pumped into the ocean, and pesticides and fertilisers from agriculture can cause toxicity and depleted oxygen levels if they enter our oceans.

!

Marine animals often mistake plastic for jelly fish and eat it, or they become entangled in it. Larger pieces of plastic break down faster in the ocean, soon becoming micro and nanoplastics. These plastics are consumed by fish and shellfish which are then eaten by humans.

OIL POLLUTION

Petroleum is used to fuel cars, boats and aircraft. It also heats homes and businesses, and is an ingredient in the asphalt needed for surfacing roads. Petroleum is pumped out of the ground or ocean floor before being transported over long distances by oil tankers. It is very toxic to any fish, plant or bird that comes into contact with it and is very difficult and expensive to clean from the ocean.

MONTARA OIL SPILL

On 21 August 2009, the Montara oil field in the Timor Sea, off the northern coast of Western Australia, suffered an event that caused an uncontrolled discharge of oil and gas into the ocean for a full 11 weeks. This resulted in Australia's worst ever oil slick. Black oil floated in the ocean and it took weeks to clean up the spill.

OTHER TYPES OF POLLUTION

While pollutants in the air and water are common, there are many other types of pollution that are not immediately visible but that have a negative impact on our lives and environment.

SOIL POLLUTION

Before people realised how dangerous toxic waste was, they would often bury it in the soil to get rid of it. Sometimes, animals eat plants that have absorbed toxins, before people eat the animals and become sick. People who have lived near landfill dumps or toxic waste sites also have higher levels of asthma and other diseases.

NOISE POLLUTION

Noise pollution is a form of air pollution that causes stress and illness, lasting damage to our hearing and even heart disease. People living near airports, main roads and construction sites commonly experience noise pollution.

POLLUTION IN SPACE

Humans have been exploring outer space and launching satellites into orbit around Earth since the late 1950s. Most of these satellites are still in space, even though they may no longer be functioning. Many space shuttles eject part of their framework during flight, and these parts are still orbiting the Earth.

It is estimated that there are more than 500,000 pieces of space debris, or junk, currently orbiting Earth. They can cause problems for other satellites or space shuttles, which would be damaged or even destroyed if they collided with space junk. The International Space Station has a special shield to protect it from space junk.

LIGHT POLLUTION

Excessive light is often produced at night in large cities, but can also be found indoors, where bright lighting may lead to worker stress and poor health. Advertising billboards, streetlights and office lights can disrupt the natural routines of animals and cause negative health effects in humans.

AGRICULTURAL POLLUTION

CHEMICAL USAGE

Farmers use a huge array of chemicals to help crops grow and to kill insects and weeds. While these chemicals may perform an important function, they also contain toxins which can cause significant damage to plant, animal and human life.

NITROUS OXIDE

Nitrous oxide is a greenhouse gas. It is emitted from pastures that have been fertilised with nitrogen.

METHANE

Methane is produced from grazing animals, mostly cows and sheep, which release methane as they digest their food. It is also released from their manure. Currently, methane accounts for 10% of Australia's total greenhouse gas pollution.

THE IMPACT OF DDT

DDT is an insecticide that was commonly used from the 1950s onwards. It was sprayed on crops to kill bugs, but was also used to control mosquitoes that caused malaria in tropical countries. DDT breaks down very slowly and remains in the environment for a long time, making its way up the food chain, stored in the fat cells of animals.

DDT causes long-term damage to animal life, particularly birds, and is also known to be highly toxic to marine life. The impact of DDT on humans is widely debated, but it is believed to increase the risk of cancer and other common diseases.

!

DDT has been completely banned in Australia since 1997 and there is now a worldwide ban on its agricultural use.

Despite the ban, it is still used in some developing countries and traces of DDT are found in many humans. Once inside the body, it is passed down to infants through their mother's breast milk.

DDT is so widespread it has even been found in Antarctic penguins.

INDUSTRY AND TRANSPORT

Coal, gas and nuclear power stations, as well as factories, produce a number of dangerous pollutants. The environmental impacts are greatest close to the original site, but there may also be long-reaching effects, such as serious marine pollution.

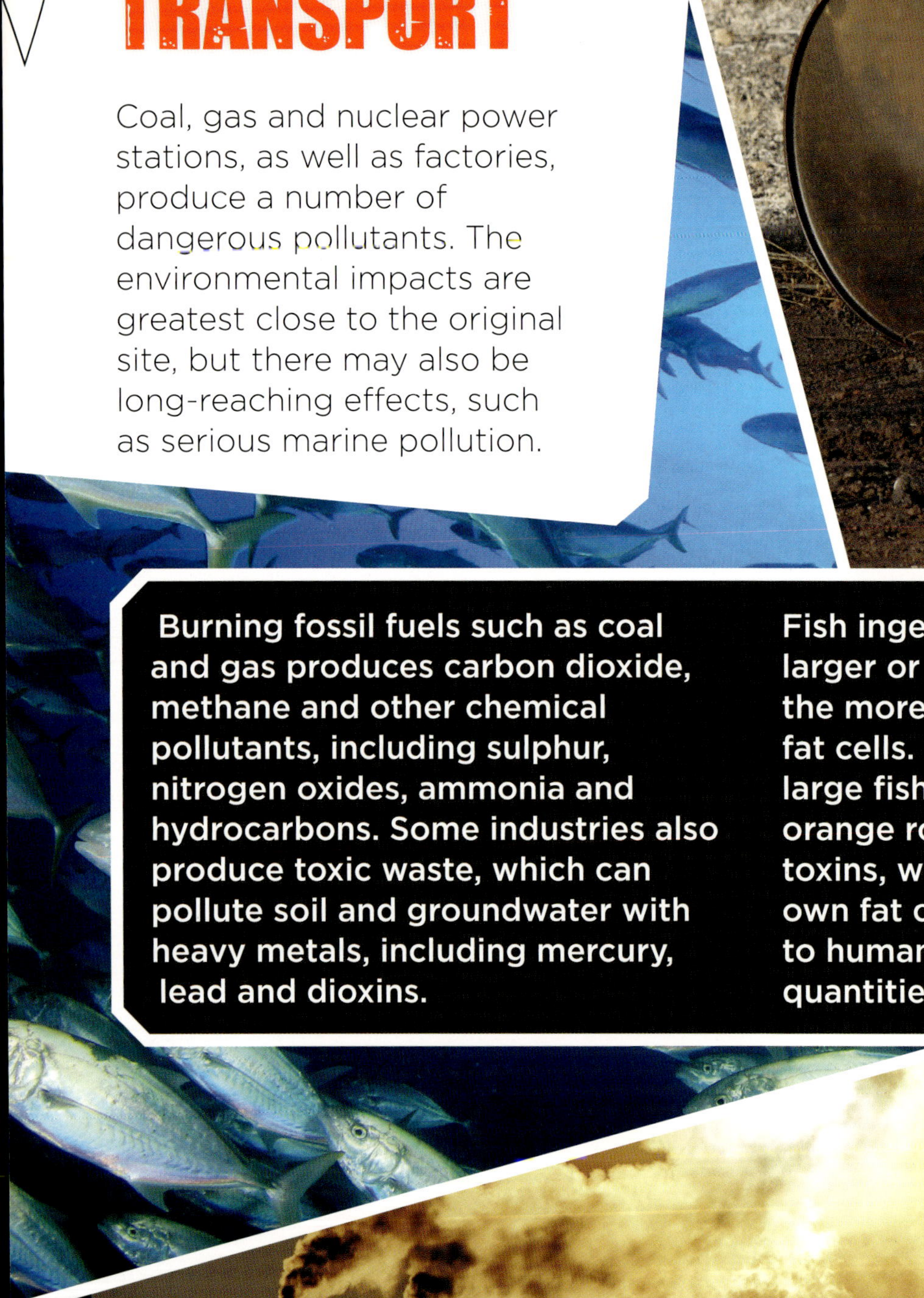

Burning fossil fuels such as coal and gas produces carbon dioxide, methane and other chemical pollutants, including sulphur, nitrogen oxides, ammonia and hydrocarbons. Some industries also produce toxic waste, which can pollute soil and groundwater with heavy metals, including mercury, lead and dioxins.

Fish ingest these toxins, and the larger or more long-lived they are, the more the toxins build up in their fat cells. When humans eat these large fish, including tuna, shark and orange roughey, we also ingest the toxins, which are then stored in our own fat cells. It can be damaging to human health if we eat large quantities of these fish.

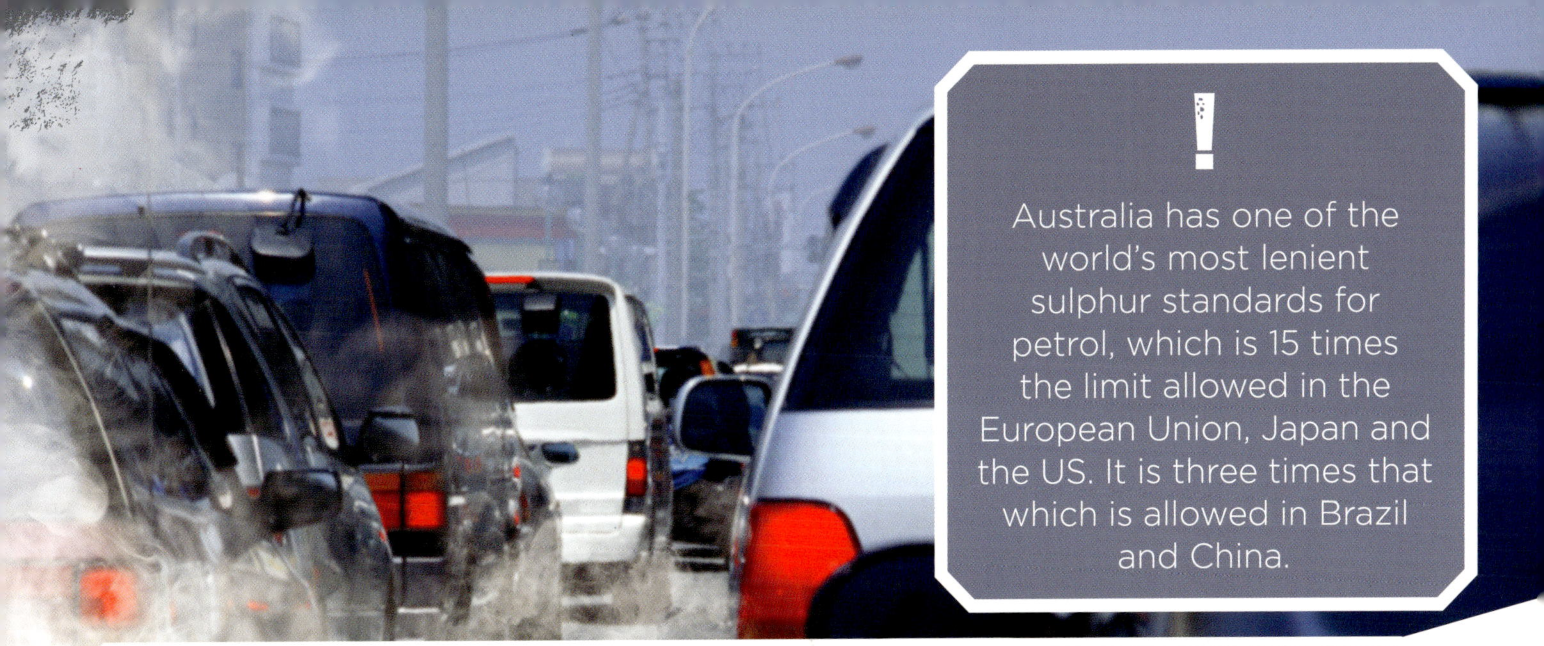

!

Australia has one of the world's most lenient sulphur standards for petrol, which is 15 times the limit allowed in the European Union, Japan and the US. It is three times that which is allowed in Brazil and China.

MOTOR VEHICLES

Australia has 19.5 million registered motor vehicles as at 31 January 2019, powered by petrol, diesel or liquid petroleum gas (LPG). Vehicles produce a number of toxic particles every time they are driven, contributing to the country's greenhouse gas emissions. They also produce dangerous air pollutants, including sulphur dioxide, nitrogen oxide, carbon monoxide, and benzene. Not only are these toxins bad for human health, but they also contribute to photochemical smog. As car tyres wear down, they release billions of micro and nanoplastics.

CLEANER CARS

As technology improves, hybrid cars are becoming less expensive and therefore more common. These cars are powered by a battery that usually needs to be plugged into the electricity grid overnight to recharge. They have a small, regular fuel tank as a backup only and could drastically reduce major pollution problems in large cities.

CLIMATE CHANGE

Climate change is already causing changes to the planet and is predicted to continue to damage our ecosystems if we don't make changes. The polar ice caps are melting, the seas are warming and their levels rising. There is an increase in extreme weather conditions such as drought and flooding. Average global temperatures are set to change and this will have an impact on farming, forests and many ecosystems.

It is likely that many plant and animal species will become extinct due to their inability to adapt to the changing climate. In Australia, we can expect less rainfall but stronger rain when it does come, along with more hot days and an increase in extreme weather events such as floods, cyclones and heatwaves.

THE GREENHOUSE EFFECT

The Earth's atmosphere is made up of a number of invisible gases, including carbon dioxide, methane, oxygen, water vapour and nitrogen. These invisible gases act like the glass of a greenhouse by allowing the sun's heat to enter the atmosphere but not allowing it to leave. This keeps the planet warm and has created what is known as the greenhouse effect.

GREENHOUSE GAS EMISSIONS

When fossil fuels, including coal, gas and oil are burned to produce power for electricity, industry and transportation, the carbon dioxide stored in the fuel is released into the atmosphere. This contributes to climate change.

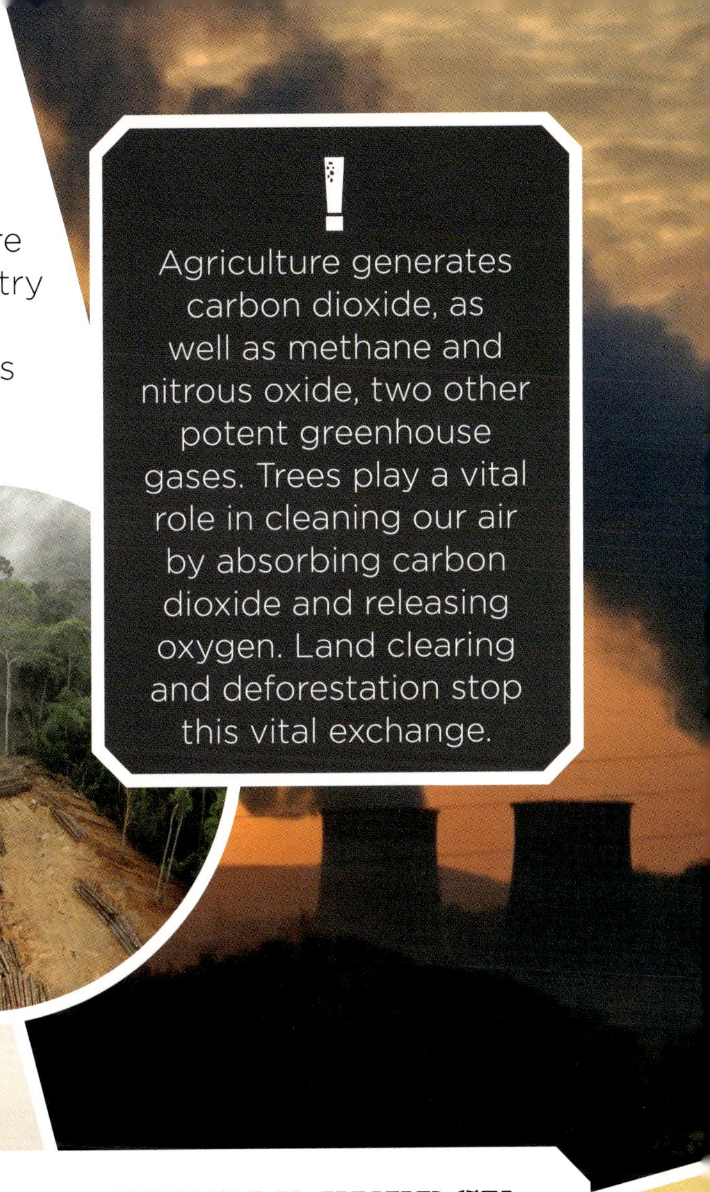

!

Agriculture generates carbon dioxide, as well as methane and nitrous oxide, two other potent greenhouse gases. Trees play a vital role in cleaning our air by absorbing carbon dioxide and releasing oxygen. Land clearing and deforestation stop this vital exchange.

RENEWABLE ENERGY

Power generation is a major contributor to air pollution and it makes sense to look towards alternative options to provide our future energy needs. Only a small portion of our electricity is currently generated by renewable resources, such as solar, wind, hydro and even burning waste from landfills. These energy sources have low running costs and do not deplete fossil fuels. Renewable energy is still a developing technology.

WHAT CAN WE DO?

There are a number of ways that everyone can help to reduce the amount of pollution in our world. The choices we make each day do make a difference and have an immediate impact on our air, soil and water.

POWER DOWN

Install renewable energy to power our homes or use the Green Power offered by our energy providers. This scheme provides a portion of your energy supply from renewable sources, at a slightly higher premium. Turn off light switches, televisions and other electrical goods when not in use.

DO NOT LITTER

Litter contributes to the pollution of our waterways and our soil. Do not litter.

CHOOSE LESS PACKAGING

Choose groceries and goods that use responsible packaging, and recycle all disposable packaging.

WALK OR USE PUBLIC TRANSPORT

Motor vehicle emissions are sources of airborne pollution.

Walking or riding a bicycle are cleaner transport choices.

Public transport produces less pollution than personal transport such as cars.

REDUCE, REUSE, RECYCLE

Significant amounts of resources are needed to make every new product. The more we can recycle products, the fewer new products need to be made and the less emissions will be generated in making them. Buying items second-hand and making sure our old household items are repaired or given away to charity help to reduce the need to manufacture new products.

GO NATURAL

Use environmentally friendly cleaning products. Washing detergents, soaps, hair shampoos and conditioners, and cleaning products contain phosphorous and other chemicals that increase the toxicity of rivers and waterways. Used chemicals, particularly motor oil and paint, should never be poured down the drain as they get into waterways and cause problems.

ENVIRONMENTAL LAW

The Environment Protection and Biodiversity Conservation Act 1999 (the EPBC Act) is the Australian Government's central piece of environmental legislation. It provides a legal framework to protect and manage nationally and internationally important flora, fauna, ecological communities and heritage places.

The National Environment Protection Council gives Australians protection from air, water, soil and noise pollution wherever they live. The Council has been responsible for controlling diesel vehicle emissions, controlling air toxins, managing contaminated land sites, identifying and transporting hazardous waste, and maintaining a national database of pollutants.

INTERNATIONAL LAWS

Over the past 30 years, major international treaties have been signed to combat the effects of ozone depletion and global warming.

One of the most successful international agreements is the Montreal Protocol on Substances that Deplete the Ozone Layer, which has been successful in removing the use of CFCs from developed countries.

GLOSSARY

atmosphere protective gases that surround Earth

carbon dioxide greenhouse gas produced by burning fossil fuels

carbon monoxide toxic gas, produced mainly by car exhausts

chlorofluorocarbon (CFC) greenhouse gas used in some aerosol cans

climate change overall changes to a climate due to changes in average temperature

contaminate to make something impure by mixing harmful impurities into it

decibels unit of measurement used to measure noise levels

deforestation chopping down forests to produce wood or to clear land

dioxins group of toxic chemicals

fossil fuels coal, oil and gas that are the ancient remains of plants and animals

global warming an increase in the overall temperature of the planet

greenhouse gases gases that trap the sun's heat. Carbon dioxide, methane, nitrous oxide

groundwater water that flows deep beneath the Earth's surface

landfill where waste is buried in large pits dug into the ground

methane greenhouse gas released by grazing cattle and at landfill sites

ozone layer layer of atmosphere that shields Earth from ultraviolet radiation

photochemical smog air, volatile organic compounds, nitrogen oxides and sunlight

recycle to process waste material so that it can be used again

sulphur dioxide polluting gas that is produced by burning coal and refining oil and gas

INDEX